JOHN LENNON

Other Books by Ken Lawrence

The World According to Michael Moore
The World According to Trump
The World According to Oprah
The World According to Bill O'Reilly

JOHN LENNON

In His Own Words

KEN LAWRENCE

**Andrews McMeel
Publishing**

Kansas City

05 06 07 08 09 FFG 10 9 8 7 6 5 4 3 2 1

ISBN-13: 978-0-7407-5477-7
ISBN-10: 0-7407-5477-7

Library of Congress Cataloging-in-Publication Data

Lawrence, Ken.
     John Lennon : in his own words / Ken Lawrence
        p. cm.
     ISBN 0-7407-5477-7
     1. Lennon, John, 1940-1980. 2. Rock musicians-England-
Biography. I. Title.
ML420.L38L33 2005
782.42166'092—dc22
[B]
                                          2005047834

Design by Kelly & Company, Lee's Summit, Missouri

ATTENTION: SCHOOLS AND BUSINESSES

Andrews McMeel books are available at quantity discounts with bulk
purchase for educational, business, or sales promotional use. For
information, please write to: Special Sales Department, Andrews
McMeel Publishing, 4520 Main Street, Kansas City, Missouri 64111.

Contents

· INTRODUCTION ·

In 1994 when the Rock and Roll Hall of Fame and Museum inducted John Lennon, they summed up his musical contribution this way: "John Lennon didn't invent rock and roll, nor did he embody it as toweringly as figures like Elvis Presley and Little Richard, but he did more than anyone else to shake it up, move it forward, and instill it with a conscience."

The museum's assessment was on the mark. As part of the Beatles, one of the world's most popular pop acts, Lennon helped shape the music scene for decades to come. Although the band sometimes was savaged by critics who considered the Beatles to be "too pop," syrupy in their love songs, and pandering to the mass audience, their fans did not care. The more the group was panned by the establishment, especially for their outlandish (for its time) long hair and clothes, the more their audience grew.

The group survived when others faded away because their music changed over time, offering ever more intriguing, thought-provoking, and complex songs. Lennon led the way on these new sounds that expanded still further when the Beatles disbanded.

As a solo artist, Lennon created music that was often socially disturbing, introspective, and even spiritual, yet it advocated a positive, hopeful vision for the future—one not always shared by other musicians during the social and cultural turmoil of the sixties and seventies. His lyrics often represented the personal turbulence he had experienced in his youth. Born October 9, 1940, Lennon was given the middle name Winston after England's Prime Minster Winston Churchill. When his parents separated, the five-year-old boy went to live with his aunt Mimi in the Liverpool suburb of Woolton. She bought him his first guitar when he was sixteen. That same year, Lennon formed a rock band, the Quarrymen, which eventually evolved into the Beatles. He was the principal singer, but he shared those duties with Paul McCartney. Even though McCartney was more pop-oriented and Lennon wrote the cutting-edge and alternative songs, the two shared songwriting credits.

Lennon had married art school classmate Cynthia Powell after she had become pregnant. They had a son, Julian, in 1963, shortly after the Beatles formed, but the marriage appeared doomed from the beginning. Their union finally broke apart when Lennon began openly dating artist Yoko Ono. The couple officially divorced in 1968 with Lennon abandoning his son—a rift that was never truly healed, according to Julian, a musician in his own right.

While his personal life was unsettled, Lennon's professional life was stellar, starting with the Beatles' debut in Hamburg, West Germany, in 1960. So pivotal was this performance in launching the group that Lennon later commented: "I grew up in Hamburg."

Back in England, the group signed Brian Epstein as their manager, and a record deal followed with George Martin as their producer.

When the Beatles began touring the world, Lennon became known as the outspoken member of the group, often the joker. Arriving in a city for a string of concerts, they gave short news conferences that were carried by TV and radio stations worldwide. Lennon was always quick with a wise-guy crack, often sarcastic and cynical about all the attention. This casual reaction to fame only spurred the group's following of ardent loyal fans.

Lennon moved beyond music, however, and published his first book, *In His Own Write,* which became an instant bestseller in March 1964. That same year, the Beatles starred in their first movie, *A Hard Day's Night,* and a year later Lennon wrote the title song, "Help!" for their movie of the same name. This song was an important touchpoint in Lennon's life as he later noted: "I didn't realize it at the time—I just wrote the song because I was commissioned to write it for the movie—but later I knew, really I was crying out for help. . . . The whole Beatle thing was just beyond comprehension. I was eating and drinking like a pig, and I was fat as a pig, dissatisfied with myself, and subconsciously I was crying for help."

Despite his dissatisfaction, the Beatles juggernaut continued on with number-one hits and sold out concerts worldwide, including one in front of 60,000 fans at New York's Shea Stadium in August 1965. They even received the prestigious honor of becoming Members of the Order of the British Empire in 1965. Lennon returned the medal to the queen several years later as part of a political protest.

Lennon often was the center of controversy, some self-constructed and some inadvertent. In 1965, London's *Evening Standard* published an interview with him in which he stated: "We're more popular than Jesus now." The remarks were taken out of context—Lennon actually meant that there were many millions more people in the world than at Jesus's time and because of television, newspapers, and radio, more people knew of the Beatles than Jesus. No matter. The remarks provoked protests in the United States on the eve of the group's 1966 tour. Radio stations refused to play their songs; the Ku Klux Klan and others burned their records and books. The protests did not affect concert attendance, and the group was as popular as ever. Lennon spent months clarifying his comments, and the Vatican accepted his apology.

Later that year, Lennon played Private Gripwood in Richard Lester's film *How I Won the War.* The movie marked his first appearance away from the group, and speculation began to circulate that the Beatles were coming apart. Although this was true, in 1967 the group released *Sgt. Pepper's Lonely Hearts Club Band,* one of its most innovative and well-received albums.

Although he was still married to Cynthia, Lennon was openly living with Yoko Ono, and they joined together for an art exhibit in London. He began to experiment with LSD and other drugs as he pulled away from the Beatles toward a new life with Ono. Many fans became angry with Ono, blaming her for discord among the Beatles. The group denied it at the time, but later it turned out to be a major factor in the breakup.

The following years were tumultuous for Lennon. He and Ono were arrested for possession of marijuana, he divorced Cynthia, and he and Ono released their album *Unfinished Music No. 1: Two Virgins,* the cover of which featured them naked. In some places the album was banned; in others it was covered in a plain wrapper.

The Beatles' last performance took place on the roof of the Apple Records building during the filming of their movie *Let It Be* on January 30, 1969. This was just a few months before Lennon and Ono married, and when John legally changed his name to John Ono Lennon. During the early days of their marriage the two engaged in bed-ins to protest violence, war, and the conflict in Vietnam in particular. Their blockbuster record "Give Peace a Chance" was recorded at the Queen Elizabeth Hotel in Montreal during one of their bed-ins. Although peace protests were common at the time, Lennon used his celebrity status to garner media attention, often using outlandish acts like the bed-in to spread his message. "We're willing to be the world's clowns if that's what it takes to promote peace," he said. But he was serious, too. His composition "Imagine," noteworthy for its gentleness and simplicity, became an anthem for many in the peace movement.

Over the next five years, Lennon released records at a fast clip including "Instant Karma" and *John Lennon/Plastic Ono Band,* his solo debut and considered by many to be his finest achievement since leaving the Beatles.

Lennon's aggressive antiwar activities captured heavy media attention and included newspaper ads and billboards in eleven cities around the world that stated: "War Is Over...If You Want It. Merry Christmas, John and Yoko." Some U.S. government officials were so frightened of Lennon's growing influence that the Senate investigated his involvement with radicals like Jerry Rubin and Abbie Hoffman, and the FBI opened a dossier that they thought would prove he was planning violent action against the country. During this time, Lennon began a four-year battle to obtain a green card. He finally received it because the FBI eventually found nothing to prevent him from becoming a permanent resident. Quoted in *Newsweek* magazine in 1976, Lennon said: "It's great to be legal. This [the United States] is where the action is." Lennon's nonincriminating FBI dossier was eventually made public—much to the embarrassment of government investigators.

Lennon continued to play concerts, but his personal life again hit a low point when he and Ono separated for eighteen months beginning in the fall of 1973. The following year he joined Elton John at Madison Square Garden in what would be his last public performance. By 1975, the Beatles were contractually unbound, and Ono and Lennon got back together. That same year, they had their first child, Sean, and Lennon's music career took a back seat as he became the house husband. Ono handled the business affairs, an unusual marriage arrangement for the time. By stepping out of the public eye for five years to raise Sean, and "watching the wheels," as he said at the time, Lennon made a public statement about the importance of family over fame.

In November 1980, Lennon and Ono released *Double Fantasy,* a month before he was shot to death by twenty-five-year-old Mark David Chapman outside their New York apartment building, the Dakota. Earlier in the day Chapman had shaken hands with Lennon and had his newly purchased copy of *Double Fantasy* autographed. Chapman said he killed Lennon because he thought it would make him important. He received a sentence of twenty years to life and has been denied parole three times. Two weeks after Lennon's death, the single "(Just Like) Starting Over" reached number one on the charts, and in 1982, *Double Fantasy* won Album of the Year for 1981.

Lennon's legacy lives on not only in the hearts of fans but in the music industry as well. In 1992, twelve years after his death, he was awarded the Lifetime Achievement Award at the Thirty-fourth Grammy Awards, and in 1998, *John Lennon Anthology*, a four-CD set of his unpublished songs and performances, was released.

In 1992, Ono told *USA Today*: "John tried to change the world with his songs."

By any measure, he succeeded.

· ON ·

THE

BEATLES

I was looking for a name like the Crickets that meant two things, and from crickets I got to "beetles." And I changed the BEA, because "beetles" didn't mean two things on its own. When you said it, people thought of crawly things, and when you read it, it was beat music.

—*LENNONlegend: An Illustrated Life of John Lennon* by James Henke

The name [Beatles] came to us in a vision.
A man descended unto us astride a flaming pie
and spake these words unto us, saying "From
this day on you are the Beatles with an A."
Thus it did come to pass thus.

—Tongue-in-cheek remark cited by the
Times (London), November 5, 1999

We were the first working-class singers that stayed working class and pronounced it and didn't try and change our accents, which in England were looked down upon.

—From *The Beatles Anthology,* cited by the
Chicago Sun-Times, December 8, 2002

And in the end, the love you take is equal to the love you make.

—On what John Lennon said was the finest line Paul McCartney ever wrote, the *Press* (Christchurch, New Zealand), June 6, 2002

Push Paul out first. He's the prettiest.

—John's comment, recalled by Victor Spinetti
of *A Hard Day's Night* while being trapped
in a limo by adoring Beatles fans,
Sunday Times (London), April 8, 2001

It would be like trying to reheat a soufflé.

—On the Beatles' getting back together,
cited by the *Toronto Star,* December 1, 1995

It's been a pleasure working with you, Ringo.

—Jokingly to Ringo during a concert after he had trashed
the band's version of "I Wanna Be Your Man," reported
by the *Independent* (London), April 16, 1992

We have a campaign to stamp out Detroit!

—When asked about the campaign in Detroit to
  "Stamp out the Beatles," as reported in the *St. Louis
  Post-Dispatch* (Missouri), October 11, 1989

I don't believe in Beatles.

—On discussing myths, review of the book
SHOUT! The Beatles in Their Generation,
the *New York Times,* April 5, 1981

Question: Why does it [your music] excite them [fans] so much?

Answer: If we knew, we'd form another group and be managers.

—First American press conference,
  JFK Airport, February 7, 1964

We're coming out in Hong Kong and suddenly you're number one there years after so many records. Even here, we've got records we've forgotten.

—News conference two days after the Beatles' American television debut on *The Ed Sullivan Show*, February 11, 1964

It wasn't until *Time* and *Life* and *Newsweek* came over and wrote articles and created an interest in us that American disc jockeys started playing our records. And Capitol said, "Well, can we have their records?" You know, they had been offered our records years ago, and they didn't want them. But when they heard we were big over here they said, "Can we have 'em now?" So we said, "As long as you promote them." So Capitol promoted, and with them and all these articles on us, the records just took off.

—Interview by Jean Shepherd in Edinburgh,
  Scotland, for *Playboy,* February 1965

We do have a bit more responsibilities than the others, you know. We [married men, Ringo and John] keep Paul and George in hand, you know.

—*Eamonn Andrews Show,* April 11, 1965

If I thought I'd got to go through the rest of my life being pointed and stared at—I'd give up the Beatles now. It's only the thought that one day it will all come to an end which keeps me going.

—*Flip Magazine,* May 1966

Ŋone of us are very sporty, you know.
The only sport we do bother with is swimming.
We don't count it as a sport, and our hobbies
are just writing songs.

—*Pop Chat*, BBC, August 1963

We don't release any more records than anybody else, it just so happens they make everything we make into a single over here [in the United States].

—Press conference, Vancouver, August 22, 1964

Well, we're no worse than bombs, are we?

—In response to whether the Beatles were a
threat to public safety, press conference,
New York City, August 28, 1964

∏ play harmonica, rhythm guitar, and vocal.
That's what they call it.

—Reportedly the Beatles' first radio interview;
  it followed the release of their first single,
  "Love Me Do," BBC, October 28, 1962

I don't want people taking things from me that aren't really me. They make you something that they want to make you, that isn't really you. They come and talk to find answers, but they're their answers, not us. We're not Beatles to each other, you know. It's a joke to us. If we're going out the door of the hotel, we say, "Right! Beatle John! Beatle George now! Come on, let's go!" We don't put on a false front or anything. But we just know that leaving the door, we turn into Beatles because everybody looking at us sees the Beatles. We're not the Beatles at all. We're just us.

—*Look* magazine, December 13, 1966

We have plenty of arguments. We're also attuned to each other. We know each other so well through the years, an argument never reaches a climax. . . . We have ordinary arguments like most people, but no conflicts.

—*Ticket to Ride* by Larry Kane, 2003

I want a divorce.

—To Paul, in fall 1969, on wanting out of the Beatles, as reported by the *Orlando Sentinel* (Florida), April 9, 1990

You have to be a bastard to make it, and the Beatles were the biggest bastards in the world!

—*Lennon Remembers*, edited by Jann Wenner

I hope he kicks himself to death.

—In response to Paul's remark that Dick Rowe of Decca Records must be kicking himself for not signing the Beatles when he had the chance, *The Beatles Come to America* by Martin Goldsmith

· ON ·

THE
FANS

The ones that are nearest.

—When asked, "Who are your most enthusiastic fans?"
press conference, New York City, August 13, 1965, two
days before the historic concert at Shea Stadium

The people that are moaning about us not being here are people that never even came to see us when we were here. We could count on our fingers the original fans we had here, and the ones that really followed us. And most of them gave up being teenagers anyway. They're all sort of settled in and different things. The ones that are moaning probably came to see us about once, or after we'd made records.

—BBC interview, Liverpool, July 10, 1964

It's [security people who keep us separated from the fans] harmed us all in the end anyway because the poor fans that have been there for twelve hours think, "Why aren't they coming to see us?"

—Press conference, Chicago, September 5, 1964

I once received a bra . . . with "I Love John" embroidered on it. I thought it was pretty original. I didn't keep it, mind you—it didn't fit.

—Asked about gifts they received from fans,
  TV interview by Larry Kane, September 13, 1964

On our last tour, people kept bringing blind, crippled, deformed children into our dressing room. This boy's mother would say, "Go on, kiss him, maybe you'll bring back his sight." We're not cruel, but when a mother shrieks, "Just touch him, and maybe he'll walk again," we want to run, cry, and empty our pockets.

—The Beatles, Fortieth Anniversary Collectors Edition,
citing 1970 interview in Rolling Stone

· ON ·

FAME

$\mathcal{A}$ woman came up and says, "I've got a so-and-so-year-old daughter." But I couldn't care less me-self. And I thought it was pretty rude, seeing as we were eating at the time as well—in the middle of a meal. So we were just a bit cold toward her. And she probably thought we had no right to be, but she forgets that we're human.

—Interview, promoting the movie
Help!, Bahamas, March 1965

We're past being bugged by questions, unless they're very personal. I mean, you just get normal human reactions to a question. You know, but there used to be one about, "What are you going to do when the bubble bursts?" and we thought we'd have hysterics because somebody always asks it.

Joe Garagiola: Let's go down the list of the questions. What are you going to do when the bubble bursts?

I haven't a clue, you know. I'm still looking for the bubble.

—*Tonight Show* with Joe Garagiola
  as substitute host, May 14, 1968

It's easier to write with cushions than on pieces of hard bench. . . . Remember, we were on hard benches before we made it in an unknown cellar in Liverpool. And it's much easier . . . on a nice cushion.

—*British Calendar News* and ITV, June 12, 1965

Well, we did that [walk freely and not be noticed] till we were about seventeen. We've had seventeen years of being able to walk to the shops. We've only had two years of not being able to walk to them.

—When asked about the downside of being famous, press conference, Melbourne, Australia, June 14, 1964

I read most newspapers all the time. Because we're often in newspapers, and it's still nice to read about yourself. And then after I've looked and seen we're not in it, then I go through the rest of it. And then I finally end up reading the political bit, when I've read everything else. I can't help being up with the times, because I am part of the times through what we've been up with, really.

—Radio interview on July 3, 1964 as part of the BBC radio program *The World of Books.* Lennon was promoting his second book, *A Spaniard in the Works.*

If you go in when the lights are down
you can go in.

—When asked if they can ever go to the movies
  without being mobbed by fans, press conference,
  Los Angeles, August 28, 1966

We just keep telling everybody that they're lousy, and hoping the kids will gradually catch on. You know, just buy 'em for the photographs and don't believe all the rubbish.

—On coverage in fan magazines, press conference,
Los Angeles, California, August 29, 1965

I thought you had to drive tanks and win wars to get the MBE.

—On receiving the Members of the Order
of the British Empire, October 26, 1965

*Y*our Majesty,

I am returning this MBE in protest against Britain's involvement in the Nigeria-Biafra thing, against our support of America in Vietnam, and against "Cold Turkey" slipping down the charts.

With Love,

John Lennon of Bag

—Letter to the queen, November 25, 1969, as cited by the *St. James Encyclopedia of Popular Culture,* 2002

· ON ·

FAMILY

Who's going to be a famous
little rocker like his dad?

—On the birth of son John Charles Julian, as reported
by the *Herald* (Glasgow, Scotland), December 7, 2000

Intellectually, of course, we did not believe in getting married. But one does not love someone just intellectually.

—In March 1969, after wedding Yoko Ono, as cited in the *Ottawa Citizen*, December 10, 1999

I'm not going to lie to [son] Julian. Ninety percent of the people on this planet, especially in the West, were born out of a bottle of whiskey on a Saturday night, and there was no intent to have children.

—On his preference for son Sean he had with Yoko Ono, from *Playboy*, January 1981, as reported by the *New York Times*, November 29, 1981

*Y*oko and I have known each other for nine years, which is a long friendship on any level. It was a long year, but it's been a nine-year relationship, a seven-year marriage. Maybe it was the seven-year crutch. And apart from the pain we caused each other it probably helped us. We knew we were getting back together, it was just a matter of when. We knew—everybody else might not have, but we did.

—On the separation from Ono,
  Hit Parader Magazine, December 1975

We're thinking it might be nice to conceive one [a child] in Amsterdam. We might call it, "Amsterdam" or "Peace" or "Hair" or "Bed-in" or something. It would be beautiful.

—During the Amsterdam bed-in, March 1969,
cited by *The Lost Beatles Interviews*

· ON ·

HAIR
AND
CLOTHING
STYLES

Question: They think your haircuts
are un-American.

Answer: Well, it was very observant of them
because we aren't American, actually.

—News conference after returning
from France, February 5, 1964

Question: There's a rumor that you fellas wear wigs.

Answer: No, we cut it ourselves.

—News conference to promote
Meet the Beatles, January, 1964

The first one we saw [capes] was in Amsterdam when we were going to these canals—some lad had one on. And we couldn't get any. You know, we could get one which wasn't the right color . . . green. We had four made in Hong Kong—copies of this one, in this material.

—Press conference, Adelaide, Australia, June 12, 1964

We just wore leather jackets. Not for the group—one person wore one, I can't remember— and then we all liked them so it ended up we were all on stage with them. And we'd always worn jeans 'cuz we didn't have anything else at the time, you know. And then we went back to Liverpool and got quite a few bookings. They all thought we were German. You know, we were billed as "From Hamburg" and they all said, "You speak good English." So we went back to Germany and we had a bit more money the second time, so we wore leather pants—and we looked like four Gene Vincents, only a bit younger, I think. And that was it, you know. We just kept the leather gear till Brian [Epstein] came along.

—BBC documentary *The Mersey Sound,* October 1963

*A*ccident . . . It just happened, you know. Ringo's was by design because he joined later.

—Asked if their haircuts were by accident or design, interview filmed at Dublin Airport, November 7, 1963

*B*oy, I wish someone had stolen our suits.

—Conversation recalled by Roger McGuinn, founding member of the folk-rock group the Byrds, on how black velvet suits he didn't like (but their manager and others in group insisted the group wear) were stolen before a show, reported in the *Orlando Sentinel* (Florida), February 21, 2003

· ON ·

HIMSELF

I'm quite normal really. If you read in the Beatle books it says I'm quite normal.

—Interview with Dibbs Mather, Doncaster, England, December 10, 1963

⊔'m not interested in being hip.

—Shortly before his death in 1980, reported
  by the *Philadelphia Inquirer*, October 29, 2004

⊔ grew up in Hamburg.

—On the city that brought the Beatles to the attention
  of the world, the *Times* (London), August 9, 2003

I didn't realize it at the time—I just wrote the song ["Help!"] because I was commissioned to write it for the movie—but later I knew, really I was crying out for help. "Help!" was about me, although it was a bit poetic. I think everything comes out in the songs. The whole Beatle thing was just beyond comprehension. I was eating and drinking like a pig, and I was fat as a pig, dissatisfied with myself, and subconsciously I was crying for help. It was my fat-Elvis period.

—From *The Beatles Anthology*, cited by the *Chicago Sun-Times*, October 1, 2000

Curse Sir Walter Raleigh, he was such a stupid git.

—On his smoking addiction, cited by
the *Guardian* (London), December 3, 1998

Part of me suspects I'm a loser, and
part of me thinks I'm God Almighty.

—Interview in *Playboy* as cited by the
Plain Dealer (Cleveland, Ohio), May 7, 1995

II consider that my work won't be finished
until I'm dead and buried.

—A radio interview several hours before his death,
  reported by the *Advertiser* (Australia), July 22, 1993

This is not how it really is. I will tell you the way it was, but nobody wants to hear it.

—Musician Van Morrison, quoting one of John's last interviews, the *Sunday Mail* (Queensland, Australia), November 25, 1990

Ⅱ don't want to grow up but I'm sick of not growing up. . . . I'll find a different way of not growing up. There's a better way of doing it than torturing your body. And then your mind. The guilt! It's just so dumb . . . I have this great fear of this normal thing. You know, the ones that passed their exams, the ones that went to their jobs, the ones that didn't become rock and rollers, the ones that settle for it, settled for it, settled for the deal! That's what I'm trying to avoid. But I'm sick of avoiding it with violence, you know? I've gotta do it some other way. I think I will. I think just the fact that I've realized it is a good step forward.

—*Rolling Stone*, June 5, 1975

Ⅱ started to put it round [as a rumor] that
I was gay. I thought that'll throw them off. I was
dancing at the gay clubs in L.A., flirting with
the boys, but it never got off.

—As recalled by Lisa Robinson, *Vanity Fair,*
November 2001

· ON ·

HIS
DRUG
USE

Reality is only for people who

can't cope with drugs.

—Cited by the *Observer* (England),
January 29, 1995

Ⅱ was all for going there and living in the Haight [Haight-Ashbury section of San Francisco], you know. I mean, in my head, I thought, "Well, hell, acid's in, so let's go. I'll go there and we'll make music and all that." But of course it didn't come true in the end. [Only] George went over.

—From the 1967 video *Beatles Anthology*, cited by the *San Francisco Chronicle*, December 12, 1995

The initials are LSD, but that's no
reference to the hallucinogen.

—On the song "Lucy in the Sky with Diamonds," insisting
it was about a picture drawn by his infant son, cited
by the *Buffalo News* (New York), May 7, 1993

Speaking as somebody who's been in the drug scene, it's not something you can go on and on doing. It's like drink or anything, you've got to come to terms with it. You know, like too much food, or too much anything. You've got to get out of it. You're left with yourself all the time, whatever you do—you know, meditation, drugs, or anything. But you've got to get down to your own god and "your own temple in your head," like Donovan [musician] says . . . it's all down to yourself.

—*Man of the Decade* interview, Associated Television Network Limited (ATV), December 30, 1969

HIS MOST
CONTROVERSIAL
QUOTE

℄hristianity will go. It will vanish and shrink. I needn't argue with that; I'm right and I will be proved right. We're more popular than Jesus now; I don't know which will go first—rock and roll or Christianity. Jesus was all right, but his disciples were thick and ordinary. It's them twisting it that ruins it for me.

—*Evening Standard* (London), March 4, 1966. The single quote, taken out of context, about the Beatles' being more popular than Jesus Christ caused a furor across the Bible Belt in the United States. Beatles records were burned, and the Ku Klux Klan burned a Beatles effigy and nailed Beatles albums to a burning cross. Lennon spent the following weeks and months clarifying what he meant.

‖ suppose if I had said television was more popular than Jesus, I would have gotten away with it. I'm sorry I opened my mouth. I'm not anti-God, anti-Christ, or antireligion. I wasn't knocking it or putting it down. I was just saying it as a fact and it's true more for England than here. I'm not saying that we're better or greater, or comparing us with Jesus Christ as a person or God as a thing or whatever it is. I just said what I said and it was wrong. Or it was taken wrong. And now it's all this.

—News conference in Chicago, August 11, 1966.
   The Vatican accepted Lennon's apology.

· ON ·

HIS
MUSIC

It's the one [song] I like best.

—On "Imagine," reported by the
Observer (England), January 7, 2001

$\coprod$'d like to say "thank you" on behalf of the group and ourselves, and I hope we passed the audition.

—Said jokingly on January 30, 1969, at the end of the fiery version of "Get Back" that the Beatles had just performed on the roof of Apple's headquarters at Three Savile Row in London's West End, cited by the *Chicago Sun-Times,* November 18, 2003

The record ["I Feel Fine"] had the first feed-back anywhere. I defy anybody to find a record—unless it's some old blues record in 1922—that uses feedback that way. I mean, everybody played feedback on stage, and the Jimi Hendrix stuff was going on long before him. In fact, the punk stuff now is only what people were doing in the clubs. So I claim for the Beatles—before Hendrix, before the Who, before anybody—the first feedback on any record.

—Cited by the *Gazette* (Montreal), September 21, 2002

I would never even dream of writing a tune like that. . . . It was only half a song [when Paul brought it to me].

—On "When I'm 64," which McCartney wrote when he was sixteen years old and both embellished for the *Sgt. Pepper* album, cited by the *Sunday Mail* (Queensland, Australia), February 3, 2002

66"In My Life," was, I think, my first real, major piece of work. Up until then, it had all been glib and throwaway. I had one mind that wrote books and another mind that churned out things about "I love you" and "you love me," because that's how Paul and I did it. I'd always tried to make some sense of the words, but I never really cared. It was the first song that I wrote that was really, consciously, about my life.

—Reported by the *Chicago Sun-Times*, October 5, 2000

I had been under obligation or contract from the time I was twenty-two until well into my thirties. After all those years it was all I knew. I wasn't free. I was boxed in. My contract was the physical manifestation of being in prison. It was more important to face myself and face that reality than to continue a life of rock and roll—and to go up and down with the whims of either your own performance or the public's opinion of you. Rock and roll was not fun anymore. I chose not to take the standard options in my business—going to Vegas and singing your great hits, if you're lucky, or going to hell, which is where Elvis went.

—*Playboy,* January 1981

started with banjo when I was fifteen when my mother taught me some banjo chords.

—*Beatles Gear: All the Fab Four's Instruments, from Stage to Studio,* by Andy Babiuk

don't know. I normally like the one we've just recorded.

—In response to, "Which song do you like best?" interview at Wembley Stadium, April 26, 1964

If I had more time I'd probably write more [books]. The publisher rang up and said, "Have you written anything yet?" and I said, "No, I've been writing songs," because I can't do both at once. You know, I've got to concentrate on the book or the songs.

—British TV show *Tonight*, June 18, 1965

After we'd done the session on that particular song ["Rain"]—it ended at about four or five in the morning—I went home with a tape to see what else you could do with it. And I was sort of very tired, you know, not knowing what I was doing, and I just happened to put it on my own tape recorder and it came out backward. And I liked it better. So that's how it happened.

—On how he began recording songs backward, press conference, New York City, August 22, 1966

So you think "Imagine" ain't political? It's "Working Class Hero" with sugar on it for conservatives like yourself!! You obviously didn't dig the words. Imagine! You took "How Do You Sleep?" so literally (read my own review of the album in *Crawdaddy* [magazine]). Your politics are very similar to Mary Whitehouse's—"Saying nothing is as loud as saying something."

—Open letter to Paul McCartney in response to his interview in *Melody Maker* magazine, November 1971

The Beatles had a standard to live up to, and for that reason, when the Beatles went into the studio, they had to stay in for at least six months. Today, I just couldn't stand to be locked up in a studio for that length of time.

—*New Musical Express,* October 7, 1972

Clive Davis once asked John Lennon what sort of music he was listening to, and was stunned by his reply: "Nothing."

"Nothing?" Davis replied. "Don't you want to know what's being played?"

"Absolutely not!" Lennon replied. "Did Picasso go to the galleries to see what was being painted?"

—*Details* magazine, December 2000

‖ thought, "What a fantastic, insane thing
to say." A warm gun means that you've
just shot something.

—After reading a caption in an American firearms magazine
that said: "Happiness Is a Warm Gun," which became the
song of the same name, as reported in *The Beatles: Every Little
Thing: A Compendium of Witty, Weird and Ever-Surprising Facts
About the Fab Four* by Maxwell MacKenzie

· ON ·

MONEY

I do have money for the first time ever, really. I do feel slightly secure about it, secure enough to say I'll go on the road for free. The reason I got rich is because I'm so insecure. I couldn't give it all away, even in my most holy, Christian, God-fearing, Hare Krishna period. I got into that struggle: I should give it all away, I don't need it. But I need it because I'm so insecure. Yoko doesn't need it. She always had it. I have to have it. I'm not secure enough to give it all up, because I need it to protect me from whatever I'm frightened of.

—*Apple to the Core* by Peter McCabe and Robert Schonfeld

Don't bother sending me all that garbage about "Just come and save the Indians, come and save the blacks, come and save the war veterans." Anybody I want to save will be helped through our tithing, which is 10 percent of whatever we earn.

—Citing *Playboy* interview, January 1981,
  the *New York Times*, November 27, 1980

It's a bit hammered now. I just keep it for kicks, really. I bought it in Germany on the HP—I remember that whatever it cost, it was a hell of a lot of money to me, at the time.

—On his first Rickenbacker guitar,
Disc Weekly, March 26, 1966

Question: Did you ever have a chance, John, to just get away on your own without anybody recognizing you?

Answer: Yeah. We borrowed a couple of millionaires' houses, you know.

Question: You could afford to BUY a couple of millionaires' houses, couldn't you?

Answer: Yeah, we'd sooner borrow 'em. It's cheaper.

—Interview in London by Pathe News
 and BBC television, February 22, 1964

OTHER MUSICIANS AND THEIR MUSIC

If there hadn't been Elvis, there would
not have been the Beatles.

—Cited by *Life,* August 1997

"Please Please Me" was my attempt at writing a Roy Orbison song.

—As reported by the *St. Louis Post-Dispatch* (Missouri), June 24, 1990

To be here now.

—Response to the question: "What is the message of rock and roll?" cited by the *Chicago Sun-Times*, August 26, 1997

The blues is a chair, not the design for a chair or a better chair. It is the first chair.

—Cited by the *Courier Mail*
(Queensland, Australia), June 13, 2003

Everything [music] comes from
everything else.

—Cited by the *Detroit News*,
February 22, 2002

Elvis died when he went into the army.

—Cited by the *Toronto Star*, January 2, 2005

We wanted to be the Goffin/King
of England.

—On writer/musician Carole King and her husband,
lyricist Gerry Goffin, as cited by the *Sunday Telegraph*
(Sydney, Australia), November 25, 2001

If you tried to give rock and roll another name, you might call it Chuck Berry.

—Reported by the *Columbus Dispatch* (Ohio), August 23, 2000

I like rock and roll, man. I don't like much else . . . that's the music that inspired me to play music. There is nothing conceptually better than rock and roll. No group, be it Beatles, Dylan, or Stones, has ever improved on "A Whole Lotta Shakin' Goin' On" for my money. That's my period and I dig it, and I'll never leave it.

—In 1971, cited by the *Sunday Mail* (Queensland, Australia), December 13, 1998

If this lasts five years, I'll be a happy man.

—When asked about the future of rock and roll,
as reported by the *Courier-Mail* (Queensland,
Australia), May 22, 1991

It hasn't been made yet.

—When asked which record he would take to
a desert island, Radio London, June 6, 1968

· ON ·

PERFORMANCES

Would the people in the cheap seats
clap your hands, and the rest of you,
if you'll just rattle your jewelry.

—Cited by the *Los Angeles Times*, May 21, 2002,
said during the Beatles' Royal Command
Performance before the queen in 1963

We never thought of miming songs at concerts—that would be cheating, wouldn't it?

—The *Age* (Australia), June 15, 1964

It's a bit chilly.

—To the crowd at the final concert by the Beatles at
Candlestick Park as the group set up behind second
base at the usually windy stadium on August 29,
1966, cited by *USA Today,* September 30, 1999

This is easily the greatest reception we've had anywhere in the world.

—On a concert stop in Adelaide, Australia, June 14, 1964, cited by the *Advertiser* (Australia), July 10, 1998

They could have taken four wax figures that looked like the Beatles, that would nod their heads at the right time, and the girls would have been happy.

—After the Beatles' last major public performance, Candlestick Park, August 29, 1966, recalled by master of ceremonies Gene Nelson, *Chicago Tribune,* August 30, 1991

We tour Europe [next]. Before America we go around Europe and see if they're still alive.

—Interviewed by Sandy Lesburgh, London, May 9, 1965

It's usually adults who don't hear 'em [the words during a noisy concert] you know—like in Hong Kong in the paper, it said, "The Beatles fought a losing battle against the screams." Now, compared with other people they were quite quiet, you know. They still shouted, and most of the kids could hear but adults point out, "I couldn't hear a thing."

—Press conference, Sydney, Australia, June 11, 1964

There's no excuses or reasons for seeing us. People keep asking questions about why they come and see us. They come and see us because they like us. That's all. There's nothing else to it, you know. And they don't have to let off steam at our concerts—they can go and let off steam anywhere.

—Press conference, Tokyo, Japan, June 30, 1966

We don't know [the tour schedule].

It's not up to us where we go.

We just climb in the vans.

—Press conference, Atlanta, Georgia, August 8, 1965

We don't expect to [see any of the city we visit while giving concerts]. We're working here. If you're at work in an office, you don't see much of the surrounding places. And it's the same for us, we don't expect to see it. If we're still alive, we'll come back when we're forty and have a look at the places that looked interesting. Last time, Ringo and I went out when we came in, it looked great. We were out in some club somewhere, I can't remember where it was, you know.

—Press conference, San Francisco, August 31, 1965

$\int$id, at Shea Stadium, I saw the
top of the mountain.

—Comment to Sid Bernstein, promoter who brought
the Beatles to Shea Stadium, as reported by
the *New York Times*, August 15, 2000

· ON ·

POLITICS

Now, I understand what you have to do: Put your political message across with a little honey. That is what most musicians fail to realize. They don't polish their messages, and as a result, they never reach the top of the charts unless it's a popular topic.

—Talking about his album *Imagine,* reported by the *Indianapolis Star,* December 26, 2003

It's great to be legal.

This is where the action is.

—On getting his green card granting him status as a U.S. resident, *Newsweek*, August 9, 1976

I think that everyone should own everything equally and that people should own part of the factories and they should have some say in who is the boss and who does what. Students should be able to select teachers. It may be like communism but I don't really know what real communism is. There is no real communism state in the world—you must realize that Russia isn't. It's a fascist state. The socialism I talk about is "British socialism," not where some daft Russian might do it or the Chinese might do it. That might suit them. Us, we'd rather have a nice socialism here—a British socialism.

—*Hit Parader Magazine,* February 1972

We're not disinterested in politics, it's just that politicians are disinteresting.

—Press conference, San Diego, California,
  August 28, 1965

Well, the communist fear is that and the American paranoia mainly, it's not too bad in Europe, it's a joke, you know. I mean, we laugh at America's fear of communists. It's like, the Americans aren't going to be overrun by communists. They're gonna fall from within, you know.

—Interview with media guru Marshall McLuhan, about John and Yoko's "War Is Over" billboard campaign, Ontario, December 19, 1969

We have this poster that says "War Is Over
if You Want It." We all sit around pointing fingers
at Nixon and the leaders of the countries saying,
"He gave us peace" or "They gave us war." But
it's *our* responsibility what happens around the
world in every other country as well as our own.
It's our responsibility for Vietnam and Biafra and
the Israel war and all the other wars we don't
quite hear about. It's *all* our responsibility and
when we all want peace we'll get it.

—Interview in Denmark 1970, cited
  by *The Lost Beatles Interviews*

Our society is driven by neurotic speed and force, accelerated by greed and the frustration of not being able to live up to the image of men and women we have created for ourselves—an image which has nothing do with the reality of people. How can we be [an] eternal James Bond or Twiggy and raise three kids on the side? So we pass our kids on to babysitters, nursery and high school teachers—three of the most underpaid positions in our society! . . . In such an image-driven culture, a piece of reality like a child becomes a direct threat to our very false existence.

—First of a regular column written by John and Yoko, *Sundance* magazine, April–May 1972

To the youth who think they are silenced by the media and alienated from the world: The future is yours. Have the patience of a pregnant woman. But don't wait for the world to reach you. You are the aware ones. Reach out. Reach out. Reach out with love. Love communicates, whereas hatred, in the end, doesn't. Extend your hand to middle America with love. There cannot be a true world revolution without the support of the silent majority.

—*Sundance*, August–September 1972

· ON ·

THE
ANTIWAR/
PEACE
MOVEMENT

If everyone demanded peace instead of another television set, then there'd be peace.

—Cited by *Guitar Player*, August 1, 2004

To struggle for peace. It is this kind of struggle. If you don't want war, there won't be war.

—As cited by the *Chicago Tribune,* January 10, 1988

We're willing to be the world's clowns,

if that's what it takes to promote peace. . . .

It was just our protest against violence.

Everybody has their bag and this is ours.

—March 1969 during their famous bed-in
when they stayed in bed at the Amsterdam
Hilton for a week to promote peace

War Is Over. . . . If You Want It.
Merry Christmas, John and Yoko

—Billboards in New York's Times Square, and other
cities throughout the world, Christmas 1969

One problem with what we're doing is that we'll never know how successful we are. With the Beatles, you put out a record and either it's a hit or a miss. I don't expect the prime ministers or kings or queens of the world to suddenly change their policies just because John and Yoko have said "Peace, brother." It would be nice, but it's the youth we're addressing. Youth is the future.

—*Lennon, the Definitive Biography* by Ray Coleman

· ON ·

THE
NEWS
MEDIA

Question: What questions would you ask yourselves if you were in our [news media] position?

Answer: I couldn't think of anything, you know. That's why we simplify so much.

—Press conference, Toronto, August 17, 1965

Some [music critics who write about us]
are intelligent, some are stupid. Some are silly,
some are stupid . . . the same in any crowd.
They're not all the same. [The magazine]
Ein is clever . . . *Ein* is soft.

—Press conference, Essen, Germany,
  June 25, 1966

· ON ·

THE
MOVIES

Most of it *[A Hard Day's Night]* was script. You can tell the script bits. They're all sort of semi-Irish/Welsh things. Most of it was script. A lot was ad-libbed.

—Press conference, Indianapolis, September 3, 1964

I don't want to make a career of it. I did it [*How I Won the War*] just 'cuz I felt like it, and Dick Lester asked me and I said "Yes." And I wouldn't have done it if the others hadn't liked it, you know. They said "fine" because we were on holiday anyway.

—ITN-TV, just outside of EMI's
  Abbey Road Studios, December 20, 1966

MISCELLANEOUS
QUOTES

Life is what happens when
you are making other plans.

—Cited by the *Australian*,
February 14, 2005

Genius is pain.

—Cited by the *Library Journal
Reviews,* July 15, 2003

Reality leaves a lot to the imagination.

—Reported by the *Sunday Herald Sun*
(Melbourne, Australia), January 19, 2003

If art were to redeem man, it could do so only by saving him from the seriousness of life and restoring him to an unexpected boyishness.

—In 1968, as cited by the *Sunday Tasmanian* (Australia), September 29, 1996

There's a great woman behind every idiot.

—As reported by *Newsday*
(New York), January 1, 1992

It takes a hypocrite to know a hypocrite.

—As reported by musician Pete Townshend,
 Playboy, February 1994

Work is life, you know, and without it, there's nothing but fear and insecurity.

—Cited by the *San Francisco Chronicle*, May 14, 1995

· ON ·

HIS
SPIRITUAL
SIDE

*M*editation gives you confidence enough
to withstand something like this, even
the short amount we've had.

—On the death of manager Brian Epstein,
August 27, 1967, press conference outside of
University College in Bangor, North Wales

There's a good guru.

—Breaking an awkward silence when meeting
Maharishi Mahesh Yogi in India and patting
him on the head, as recalled by musician
Donovan, *Los Angeles Times,* August 6, 1991

hat's the whole game. There's no other time but the present. Anything else is a waste of time. Like Yoko says, most people spend so much time trying to be proper, they waste all their energy. People wonder where we get all our energy from. We're like children; we don't spend any time trying to be proper.

—*Melody Maker*, October 2, 1971

It's true we can do with a few big miracles right now. The thing is to recognize them when they come to you and to be thankful. First they come in a small way, in everyday life, then they come in rivers, and in oceans. It's goin' to be alright! The future of the earth is up to all of us. Many people are sending us vibes every day in letters, telegrams, taps on the gate, or just flowers and nice thoughts. We thank them all and appreciate them for respecting our quiet space, which we need. Thank you for all the love you send us. We feel it every day.
We love you, too.

—A love letter from John and Yoko,
  the *New York Times*, May 27, 1979

Listen, Brother, Why don't you Jesus Freaks
get off people's backs?

It's been the same for two thousand years—won't
you ever learn? Those who know do not speak.
Those who speak do not know. Your peace of
mind doesn't show in your neurotic letter, son.

One man's meat—brother!

Peace off! John + Yoko.

—Letter written in 1971 in response to a missive from Tom
Bonifield of Lexington, Kentucky, who was troubled by the
lyrics "Imagine there's no heaven. . . ." The letter sold at
auction for $3,300, as reported by *People Weekly,* July 19, 1993

It seems to be the law of the universe, that as you move forward you must move something back. Like I spent a lot of time teaching her [Yoko's] ex-husband a few chords on the guitar and the reward's gonna be I'm gonna learn a few more tricks on the guitar. It's as simple as that to me. Do unto others bit. And whatever you've found out, you've got to pass it on to your next of kin to make your next move up.

—*Hit Parader Magazine*, August 1970

He [Mahesh Yogi] wasn't a farce. I still meditate now and then. I just found that I couldn't do it every day. It's like exercising, you know. I couldn't get up and touch me toes every day. But the meditation was good and the three months in India produced all those songs in the double album, not the fact that I was in India, the fact of what I was doing, the meditation and how I felt. So they all thought he conned us out of money. He never got a penny out of us.

—*T.O. Magazine*, December 1988

WHAT OTHERS SAY ABOUT HIM

John tried to change the world with his songs.

—Wife Yoko Ono, *USA Today,* November 13, 1992

He would definitely have continued to play music. Who knows, he might have toured with Sean and Julian. . . . I do think he would have continued to paint and write. Music was just one part of his genius. He was truly multitalented and would have written his autobiography and maybe other books which would have been best sellers. He was also a wonderful artist.

—Julia Baird, one of his three half-sisters, the
  Scotsman (Edinburgh, Scotland), October 8, 2004

Boxer Cassius Clay, soon to be known
as Muhammad Ali, acknowledged something
John Lennon had said by saying:
"You ain't as dumb as you look."

"No. But you are," said John, joking.

—Robert Lipsyte, sportswriter for the *New York Times*,
at the Fifth Street Gym the day of the Beatles' visit,
as reported by the *Irish Times*, February 21, 2004

I went to New York and photographed him and Yoko [Ono], and it was such a great experience because he was one of the Beatles. But he immediately set me at ease and taught me this wonderful lesson about just being yourself and playing it as straight as you can. It stuck with me forever, and I sort of expected the same from everyone and myself—just to be yourself.

—Celebrity photographer Annie Leibovitz on one of her first shoots for *Rolling Stone* magazine, the *San Diego Union-Tribune*, November 23, 2003

Even if it was cyanide, I would have drunk it.

—Maurice Gibb, member of the Bee Gees, interviewed in 2001, on John Lennon giving him his first scotch when he was seventeen, *Toronto Star,* January 13, 2003

𝕁ohn Lennon was held in great affection in his home city. We want to build on that tribute by continuing to grow the airport that bears his name.

—Neil Pakey, commercial director of Peel Holdings, owners of the Liverpool Airport, renamed Liverpool John Lennon Airport, the *Independent* (London), July 3, 2001

After that [when John left his wife Cynthia and son Julian] I only saw him a handful of times before he was killed. Sadly, I never really knew the man. I had a great deal of anger toward dad because of his negligence and his attitude to peace and love. That peace and love never came home to me. . . . Once I began to look at his life and really understand him, I began to feel so sorry for him, because once he was a guiding light, a star that shone on all of us, until he was sucked into a black hole and all of his strength consumed. Although he was definitely afraid of fatherhood, the combination of that and his life with Yoko Ono led to the real breakdown of our relationship.

—Son Julian in the *Herald* (Glasgow, Scotland), December 7, 2000

The Beatles were formative in my upbringing, my education. They came from a very similar background—the industrial towns in England, working class; they wrote their own songs, conquered the world. That was the blueprint for lots of other British kids to try to do the same. We all miss him [John], and I think about him every time I walk by that building [the Dakota, where he was shot].

—Sting in the *Observer* (England), December 3, 2000

When the Beatles were offered the song "How Do You Do It," they didn't like it. John said to Brian Epstein, "That's a really lousy, terrible song. Why don't you give it to Gerry, he'll do it." I still thank him in my prayers for my first number one.

—Gerry Marsden, of Gerry and the Pacemakers,
the *Times* (London), December 2, 2000

I'd try to lead an ordinary life . . . stay out of the papers. There's not too many places to go once you've killed someone like John Lennon.

—Mark David Chapman, on what he would do if he was released from prison, the *Australian,* October 2, 2000

John Lennon is a very large industry. There are greeting cards, glasses, hats, T-shirts, tote bags, and even barbecue aprons, but it denigrates him. This crass, gross merchandising in the name of John Lennon is a deep and great shame. We would be better off knowing the truth about this great artist, that he was a disturbed, twisted, emotionally retarded, wonderful genius.

—Geoffrey Giuliano, author of *Lennon in America*,
the *Herald* (Glasgow, Scotland), April 19, 2000

Ⅱ can't tell you how many times I've walked into a store or mall and heard my dad singing. I just get this really nice feeling, as if he's saying, "Hey, how are you?" or "I'm still around." It's almost magical.

—Son Julian Lennon in *Jump* magazine, cited by the *Gazette* (Montreal), December 14, 1998

When we were kids we always used to say, "OK, whoever dies first, get a message through." When John died, I thought, "Well, maybe we'll get a message," because I know he knew the deal. I haven't had a message from John.

—Paul McCartney, *Tampa Tribune* (Florida), December 10, 1997

But he had a good married relationship with [John's first wife] Cynthia. It was when drugs came on the scene that things went wrong. The women in my family are all strong creatures. John was very weak and Cynthia wasn't strong enough for him. John wanted his mother and he replaced her with Yoko.

—John's half-sister Julia, *Courier Mail* (Queensland, Australia), March 30, 1996

None of us [the Beatles] ever got taught music, and John Lennon never passed an exam in his life.

—Paul McCartney, *Herald Sun* (Australia), December 31, 1990

It is so sad to watch this movie. It is about the life and death, the poetry, and the music of a very important man. For me, it is very emotional.

—Cynthia Lennon, on the movie *Imagine: John Lennon,* the *Advertiser,* November 10, 1988

It is John. He was a very complex person and all aspects of his emotions and his life have been covered. You will see from all different angles what John really was about.

—Yoko Ono, *Imagine: John Lennon*,
the *Toronto Star*, October 2, 1988

We don't like their sound.
Groups of guitars are on the way out. . . .

—Officials of the Decca Recording Company
rejecting an opportunity to sign the Beatles
to a long-term contract, 1962, as reported
in *The Book of Heroic Failures* by Stephen Pile

Visually they are a nightmare. . . .
Musically they are a near disaster, and the
lyrics punctuated by nutty shouts of "yeah,
yeah, yeah" are a catastrophe, a preposterous
farrago of Valentine-card romantic sentiments.

—*Newsweek* magazine's review of the Beatles'
appearance on *The Ed Sullivan Show* in 1964, as
cited by the *New York Times*, March 1, 2004

He has too many of the wrong ambitions, and his energy is too often misplaced.

—Headmaster on John Lennon's report card,
  summer of 1956, when Lennon was fifteen,
  reported by *Rolling Stone*, February 19, 2004

I was feeling like I was worthless, and maybe the root of it is a self-esteem issue. I felt like nothing, and I felt if I shot him, I would become something, which is not true at all.

—Mark David Chapman at his
October 3, 2000, parole hearing